LUCAS
Plays

By Christina Shawn
Illustrated by Shawn Yu

For Madelyn, Lucas, and Aubrey,
May you always love to play.

A special thank you to my husband,
RJ, for believing in me,
motivating me, and supporting me,
every step of the way.

-C.S.

First Edition - November 2017

Library of Congress Control Number: 2017915640
ISBN: 978-0-692-93745-7

Graphic Design: Elizabeth Baroody - EEBDesigns, LLC

Summary:
As Lucas plays the violin, his world of traditional play (toy cars, superhero figurines, tire swings, and sand castles)
transforms into one of imagination, with quirky aliens and snoring monsters. This book appeals to the
cheerful whimsy of children at play, as well as the magic and wonder of music.

LUCAS Plays

By Christina Shawn
Illustrated by Shawn Yu

Lucas plays!
He plays and plays and
plays and plays and plays.

He plays cars,
and monsters,
and superheroes,
and space invaders.

He plays in the ocean,
and in the sand,

and in the mud,
and in the trees.

Lucas loves to play,
and what he loves to play most is his violin.

He loves to make music with the wood and the strings,
and imagine the world as his violin sings.
Every stroke of the bow, every way that he plays,
creates a new world he can dream in for days.

And each group of notes
forms a story, you see,
with alien spaceships,
or monkeys in trees.

He listens for waves that crash to the shore,
stirring up seashells from the sea floor.

He listens for monsters parading through towns,
with purplish hair and bright golden crowns.

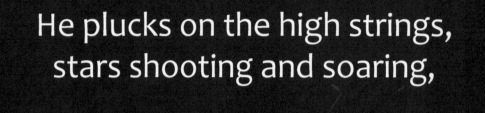

He plucks on the high strings,
stars shooting and soaring,

and vibrates the low strings
like great monsters snoring!

He plays the notes long, drawn out and slow,
like dragging your feet through the mud or the snow.

He plays the notes short, fluttering and quick,
like jumping in leaves or kicking up sticks.

He transforms the world of
what's real and what's true,
to his vision of something
exciting and new.

Three high notes ring out and a hero appears!
He saves the whole world and everyone cheers!

Now eight low notes rumble, trees quiver and shake!
A spaceship has landed, down there! By the lake!

And then there's the quirkiest sound of them all,
four green-spotted aliens, seven feet tall!

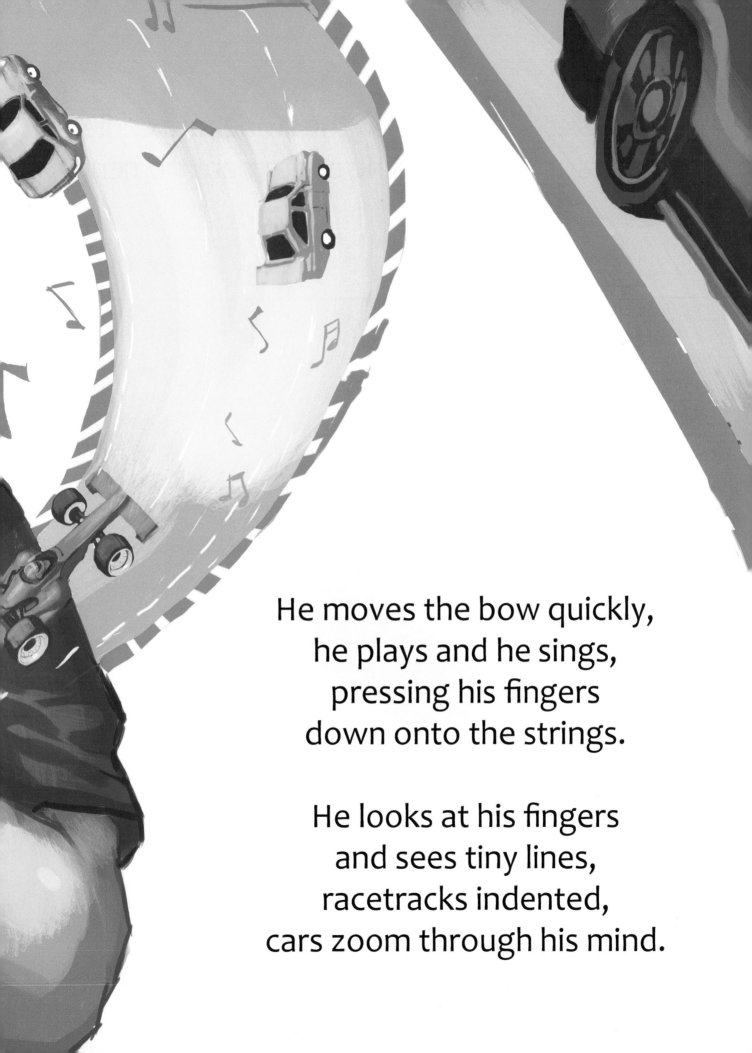

He moves the bow quickly,
he plays and he sings,
pressing his fingers
down onto the strings.

He looks at his fingers
and sees tiny lines,
racetracks indented,
cars zoom through his mind.

The notes are abundant, the stories are endless.
The characters thrilling, the excitement tremendous!

Notes dance off the strings and run off the bow,
paint the room orange, make the room glow.

Tunes swell in his heart and rattle his bones.
They prickle his skin and tickle his toes.
He smiles as he plays his best notes again!
His giggles escape, his heart flips and spins!

He plays loudly,
and softly,
and quickly,
and slowly.

Lucas loves to play!
He plays and plays and
plays and plays and
plays.